Lon

CW00348955

Improve Your Word Power

Sue Lloyd

Longman

INTRODUCTION

Do you often find yourself at a loss for words? Is your written work flat and uninteresting? Do you fail to put your ideas (and yourself) across at interviews? A knowledge of the English language can give you confidence and help you to express yourself clearly and effectively.

This little book takes eighty groups of words dealing with common topics, and shows you how to use them in your speaking and writing. Each group has a heading, usually the most general word in the group, and each offers you:

a list of words with similar meanings
an explanation of each word's particular meaning
an example of the use of each word
a list of contrasting words, if there are any.

So under each heading, you will find a variety of ways of expressing the same idea. The explanations and examples will help you to choose the best word for your purpose, and your writing and speaking will become more effective as a result.

Let's assume you have thought of a word, but you need a better one. Find the group where your word is dealt with by looking it up in the Word Finder at the back of the book. Here every word discussed is listed along with the number of the group where it can be found.

Small as it is, this book offers you guidance on how to use over 600 words, and suggests, too, many contrasting words. For an even greater choice, you need a thesaurus, and we have added a brief course in how to use one at the end.

Sue Lloyd

ACT (1)

Act, action, deed, exploit and **feat** may all mean something done.

act: the emphasis is on what was done
> an **act** of kindness that was never forgotten

action: here the emphasis is on the doing instead
> **action** speaks louder than words; take **action** now!

actions, deeds: conduct or behaviour
> these were the **actions** of a good man; noble **deeds**

deed: a notable or praiseworthy act; used nowadays usually in the phrase 'good **deed**'

exploit: a deed displaying physical courage or heroism
> the **exploits** of Airwoman Anderson

feat: a deed of great physical or mental skill or daring
> acrobatic **feats**; a **feat** of memory

ACTIVE (2)

Active, the opposite of lazy, suggests constant movement and activity: an **active** life; still **active** at eighty. (See also **QUICK**.) Similar words are:

lively: full of life and energy
> three **lively** daughters; a **lively** discussion

animated: spirited and energetic
> the conversation became more and more **animated**

vivacious: bright and lively in manner
> a **vivacious** young horsewoman

sprightly: moving easily and quickly with youthful energy
> he is surprisingly **sprightly** for his age

dynamic: full of driving energy
> a **dynamic** young business executive

Contrast: **lazy, idle, indolent; listless, lethargic**

ADMIRE (3)

Admire, approve, respect and **esteem** all mean to recognise the worth of something.

approve: (the weakest) to have or express a favourable opinion of someone or something
*she **approved** of his new suit*
admire: to feel and express wonder and approval
*everyone **admired** the splendid display of flowers*
respect: (of people) adds a sense of deference but not necessarily liking
*I **respect** her courage but dislike her attitude*
esteem: (of people) adds affection to respect
*we shall be sorry to lose such an **esteemed** colleague*

Contrast: **disapprove of, despise, scorn**

ANGER (4)

Anger: feeling and usually expressing strong displeasure: *could not contain her **anger***. Compare:

indignation: justly provoked anger, deeply felt
***indignation** at being passed over for the job*
resentment: a brooding, contained anger due to a sense of grievance
*this unfair treatment caused much **resentment***
rage: vehemently expressed anger
*he flew into a **rage** for no reason at all*
fury: stronger than rage; almost mad with anger
*in her **fury**, she burnt all his letters*

Contrast: **calmness, coolness, self-control**

ANNOY (5)

Annoy: to cause anger or impatience and often dislike: *his constant whistling **annoyed** her.* Compare:

bother: a milder word for slight annoyances or interruptions
> *don't **bother** me now, I'm busy; does my radio **bother** you?*

pester: to keep bothering someone
> *the child was **pestering** her parents for an ice*

harass: to relentlessly cause worry and annoyance
> *they were **harassed** by clouds of mosquitoes*

irritate: to annoy someone, often in a trivial way, so that they lose their patience or good humour
> *she **irritated** her parents by humming at mealtimes*

provoke: to cause resentment, often deliberately
> *he was **provoked** by her apparent lack of interest*

vex: stronger than 'provoke', and causing deeper feelings
> *his failure to keep the appointment **vexed** her greatly*

nettle: to cause temporary irritation, often by an attack on someone's self-esteem
> ***nettled** by their comments on her appearance, she went to have her hair done*

exasperate: to annoy people so much that they lose their patience or their temper
> *the students **exasperated** the teacher by failing to hand in their work on time*

infuriate: stronger than 'exasperate'; to annoy to the point of (usually impotent) rage
> *the noise from the disco **infuriated** the neighbours*

ANXIETY (6)

Anxiety: an unsettled and uneasy state of mind: ***anxiety*** *about her father*. Similar words include:

worry: persistent, nagging fears and doubts, sometimes unnecessary or out of proportion
*his children are a **worry** to him; forget your **worries***
misgiving: suspicions and uncertainty about the result of some action or event
*in spite of my **misgivings**, I lent him the car*
disquiet: vague and mild uneasiness
*their **disquiet** soon turned into real fear*
apprehension: nervous anxiety about the future
*we waited with **apprehension** for the exam results*
dread: helpless terror about what might happen
*a **dread** of the dark; **dread** of a nuclear war*

See also: **FEAR.** Contrast: **calmness, confidence, equanimity**

APPROPRIATE (7)

Appropriate: particularly right for the occasion: *the **appropriate** form; an **appropriate** greetings card.* Often interchangeable with:

suitable: milder and more general than the others
*help me to find a **suitable** tie for the interview*
fitting: very appropriate
*we gave the hero a **fitting** welcome*
apt: suitable because skilfully chosen
*a speech full of **apt** quotations*
proper: suitable by its nature or social custom
*everything in its **proper** place; show a **proper** respect*
fit for: suitable for what is named
*a robe **fit for** a queen*

Contrast: **unsuitable, inappropriate, out of place**

BAD-TEMPERED (8)

Bad-tempered: describing someone habitually or temporarily out of humour: *always **bad-tempered** at breakfast.* Similar words include:

grumpy: bad-tempered, cross or unsociable
> *the **grumpy** waitress took our order with a frown*

gruff: not very forthcoming or friendly; rough or brusque in speech or manner (usually describing men)
> *his **gruff** manners hide a kind heart*

surly: gruff and irritable to the point of rudeness
> *the **surly** gamekeeper shouted curses after us*

sullen: stubbornly gloomy, resentful and unsociable
> *the **sullen** girl's face was transformed by a smile*

sulky: tending to sulk; sulking and moody
> *no one likes **sulky** children – so cheer up!*

peevish: easy to upset; always finding fault
> ***peevish** diners who complain the food is cold*

petulant: childishly bad-tempered; irritably impatient, especially over unimportant things
> *that **petulant** young man has been spoilt by his rich parents*

irritable: easily annoyed
> *why are you so **irritable** today?*

irascible: habitually quick to lose one's temper
> *the **irascible** old housekeeper told us off for smoking in the bedroom*

cantankerous: bad-tempered and quarrelsome
> *my boss is rather **cantankerous**, but he pays me well*

cross: (often) angry, annoyed or in a bad mood
> *I'm always **cross** on Mondays*

Contrast: **good-tempered, cheerful, easy-going, sociable, genial, jolly, jovial, sanguine**

BEAUTIFUL (9)

The following words all describe what is pleasant to look at:

beautiful: very satisfying to the senses and the mind; approaching perfection
*a **beautiful** painting; **beautiful** lilies; a **beautiful** woman*

lovely: emotionally satisfying as well as delightful to the senses
*her **lovely**, kind face; the lake looked **lovely** in the evening light*

pretty: suggests a smaller scale and a less deeply felt experience than 'lovely' and 'beautiful'
*a **pretty** little cottage; a **pretty** face*

handsome: unlike the three preceding words, this can be used of men as well as women and suggests dignity and attractively regular or striking features
*a **handsome** woman in her fifties; her **handsome** husband; **handsome** Regency terraces*

elegant: graceful and dignified; (of women) carefully and becomingly dressed and groomed
*a fine table with **elegant** curving legs; **elegant** models*

exquisite: delicately beautiful
***exquisite** lace shawls; an **exquisite** face, perfect in every feature*

picturesque: (of landscapes, buildings) charming to look at; quaint or appealing
***picturesque** thatched cottages*

Contrast: **unsightly, unattractive, plain; ugly, hideous, repulsive, grotesque**

BEGIN (10)

Begin: (the opposite of 'end') to take the first steps in doing something: *they want to **begin** singing lessons; she **began** to sing; let's **begin**.* Very similar are:

commence: a more formal word for 'begin'
　　*the new term **commences** on 1st October*
start: as the opposite of 'stop', it stresses the fact of beginning some activity or setting out from a particular point for a particular purpose
　　*it **started** to rain; we **started** out*
initiate: to be the person who starts something off
　　*our teacher **initiated** the penfriend scheme last year*

Contrast: **END**

BENEFICIAL (11)

Beneficial: describes what is good for you, especially for your physical or mental health; *the **beneficial** influence of sunshine.* Similar words include:

advantageous: something which gives you an advantage
　　*it is **advantageous** to have a good education*
profitable: worthwhile in terms of earning money or learning from experience
　　*a **profitable** day's work; a **profitable** lesson in humility*
favourable: describes something which furthers your purposes or suggests future advantages
　　*a **favourable** wind blew them to France; a **favourable** report of future business trends*

Contrast: **harmful, damaging, detrimental, adverse**

BRAVE (12)

Brave: resolutely facing danger without, or in spite of, fear: *brave rescuers tunnelling into the rubble of the earthquake; a brave action*. Similar words include:

courageous: stressing moral or mental strength
> *a courageous struggle against cancer; courageous volunteers needed for mountain rescue work*

valiant: suggests bravery in the face of insuperable dangers or difficulties
> *in spite of her valiant attempts to reach him, the child died in the fire; our valiant troops*

valorous: describes brave deeds, or the spirit which prompts them
> *a valorous disregard for his own safety*

heroic: showing noble and selfless bravery and daring worthy of a hero or heroine
> *heroic efforts; heroic men and women pioneers*

gallant: chivalrous, valiant and heroic
> *gallant attempts; a gallant knight*

intrepid: fearless and self-possessed
> *the intrepid explorers pressed on into the jungle*

dauntless: resolutely fearless; not intimidated
> *Jack the dauntless Giant-killer*

plucky: (informal) brave against all the odds
> *a plucky lass who never gave in to despair*

Bold suggests a willing exposure to danger and readiness to take risks which may not always be wise: *a bold plan; bold adventurers*. Like **bold** are:

audacious: stronger than bold, may imply ingenious daring
> *an audacious burglar stole the ring as she slept*

foolhardy: reckless boldness to the point of foolishness
> *a foolhardy attempt to swim the swollen river*

Contrast: **cowardly, fainthearted, timid, fearful; cautious, prudent**

BRIGHT (13)

Bright: radiating or reflecting light: *a **bright** day; **bright** lights.*
Compare:

brilliant: stronger than bright, almost dazzling
    *   **brilliant** sunshine; **brilliant** diamonds*
radiant: giving out a steady, intense and joyous brightness
    *   a **radiant** April morning; **radiant** faces*
luminous: glowing, often in the dark, or shining through
    something translucent
    *   **luminous** rubies; the **luminous** eyes of a cat at night*
lustrous: reflecting light off a smooth, shiny surface
    *   the **lustrous** coat of a well-fed spaniel*
vivid: (often with colours) intensely, glaringly bright
    *   a **vivid** red dress*

See also: **SHINE**. Contrast: **dim, dark, dull**

CAREFUL (14)

C

Careful: paying close attention; guarding against mistakes;
thorough and cautious: *a **careful** check; **careful** writers; be
careful on the road.* Compare:

painstaking: paying careful attention to details
    *   a **painstaking** account of what happened*
conscientious, scrupulous: being careful as a matter of
    conscience or duty
    *   a **conscientious** worker; **scrupulous** reporting*
meticulous: paying close attention to details
    *   the show's success was due to **meticulous** planning*
diligent, assiduous: consistently and painstakingly careful
    *   a **diligent** study of documents; an **assiduous** listener*

Contrast: **careless, negligent, slapdash, remiss**

CLEVER (15)

Clever: very intelligent; showing great ingenuity and resourcefulness: *a **clever** girl who is going to university; a **clever** plan*. Other words suggesting intelligence include:

bright: (usually used of young people) lively, alert, keen and quick to learn
   bright children who are a pleasure to teach; a bright remark
brilliant: outstandingly **clever** in a particular subject
   she is a brilliant mathematician; brilliant reasoning
quickwitted: quick to think and act, especially in a difficult situation
   the quickwitted thief escaped through the window; a quickwitted reply
perceptive: able to interpret situations intelligently, and to understand and notice things, particularly human behaviour and emotions
   it was perceptive of you to see she needed a rest; a perceptive study of old age
shrewd: using one's intelligence to sum up a situation correctly in order to take advantage of it
   a shrewd businessman who made a fortune; a shrewd deal
astute: like 'shrewd', but without the suggestion of selfishness
   the astute lawyer saw that the witness was lying; an astute observation

See also: **SKILFUL.**
Contrast: **stupid, dull, dense, slow, backward**

CRY (16)

Cry is a general term for expressing sorrow, pain or fear in sounds and/or tears: *we **cried** when our hamster died*. Other words which can have similar meanings are:

weep: (formal) stresses the shedding of tears
      *they **wept** bitterly by the graveside*
sob: to gasp and catch your breath as you weep
      *I can't go on, he **sobbed** despairingly*
sigh: to express sadness and other emotions in a long, deep, audible breath
      *she thought of her sad secret and **sighed***
groan: to give a long, low sigh of sorrow or pain
      *the injured soldier lay **groaning***
moan: to groan mournfully and pathetically
      *she **moaned** as the pain came again*
howl: to cry very loudly and unrestrainedly
      *he **howled** like a child at the news*
bawl: like howl, but more critical
      *she's **bawling** because she fell and grazed her knee*
whimper: to give little broken, pathetic cries (often used of frightened children or animals)
      *the lost child was found **whimpering** in the street*
wail: to give a long, high-pitched, mournful cry
      *the child woke up and **wailed** for its parents*
yell: to give a very loud cry of shocked pain, fear, etc.
      *he **yelled** as the needle went into his arm*
scream: to let out a loud, high-pitched and piercing cry of pain or fright
      *she **screamed** as the assassin turned to shoot*
shriek: shorter and shriller than scream
      *do you **shriek** when you see a large spider?*

Contrast: **LAUGH; rejoice, exult**

CUT (17)

Cut: a general term meaning to open up or divide with something sharp: *I cut my finger; cut the cake.*
The following words give more information:

slash: to make an imprecise cut with a wild and violent blow
   slashed the cushions so that the stuffing fell out
hack: to make repeated but crude attempts to cut
   they hacked the block of marble with their axes
slice: to divide something with a precise cut
   to slice off the top of an egg; to slice bread
slit: to make a long, narrow, straight cut or opening
   to slit open an envelope; to slit material to make a buttonhole
gash: to make a long, deep, often irregular cut
   she gashed her finger on a nail
notch: to make a small sharp V-shaped cut, often as a marker
   they notched the trees as they went to mark the way
chop: to cut down, often with repeated blows, using an axe, etc.; to cut up into pieces
   chop down that tree; chop up the carrots
hew: to shape or cut with heavy blows
   hew the marble into shape; hew down the tree
split: to divide with a cut along the grain
   split logs for the fire
cleave: (written) to divide or split something hard with a violent blow
   he cleaves the rock with his sacred staff
sever: to separate from the main part of something with a short, sharp cut
   the executioner's sword severed the queen's head
dissect: to take something apart by cutting, in order to examine its structure
   we dissected a dead locust in school today

CRUEL (18)

Cruel: indifferent to, or willing to cause, pain and suffering: *cruel parents; a cruel remark.* Compare:

brutal: inhuman, insensitive, even physically violent
    brutal treatment; a brutal murderer
savage: fierce, wild and brutal
    seas infested by savage pirates; a savage storm
sadistic: taking pleasure in being cruel
    a sadistic delight in torturing beetles
harsh: cruel, unfeeling, severe
    a harsh punishment; a harsh prison warder
pitiless: showing no pity or compassion
    the pitiless conqueror killed even the children
ruthless: hardhearted and unscrupulous
    the ruthless dictator had his enemies assassinated

Contrast: **KIND**

DANGER (19)

D

Danger: a situation which poses a risk of harm: *the danger of skating on thin ice; a danger to the public.* Similar words include:

peril: great danger, with injury or death possible
    in peril of one's life; the perils of potholing
pitfall: a hidden source of danger; a trap
    the pitfalls of appearing on television
hazard: possible danger due to chance and beyond control
    ice is a hazard on the roads this morning
risk: a milder term than the others, suggesting dangers you
    are willing to face for good reasons
    ask yourself, is it worth the risk?

Contrast: **safety, security; harmlessness**

DIFFICULT (21)

Difficult: requiring mental or physical effort; posing problems only to be overcome by intelligence, skill, etc.: *a **difficult** question to answer; **difficult** exercises.* Similar words are:

hard: a more general and informal term, contrasted with 'easy'
　　*a **hard** job; a **hard** decision; **hard** exams*
tough: very difficult and often physically demanding
　　*a **tough** climb; it was a **tough** life in the outback*
arduous: calling for exertion, perseverance and stamina
　　*an **arduous** mountaineering expedition; an **arduous** task*
perplexing: difficult to understand or act upon
　　*a **perplexing** telephone call from a stranger; spent a **perplexing** half-hour trying to balance the accounts*

Contrast: **easy, effortless, undemanding; OBVIOUS**

DIRTY (22)

Dirty: covered in dirt; not clean or tidy: *a **dirty** apron; **dirty** feet; a **dirty** floor.* Stronger words include:

grimy: covered with dirt, especially ingrained dirt
　　*a **grimy** coalminer; **grimy** wallpaper*
squalid: offensively dirty, often because of poverty or neglect
　　*a **squalid** bedsitter; **squalid** children in rags*
sordid: like 'squalid', but adding a moral judgement
　　*our **sordid** slums encourage crime*
foul: revoltingly dirty, because smelly or polluted
　　***foul** sewers; **foul** alleyways*
filthy: excessively dirty (a very critical term)
　　*take those **filthy** shoes off before you come inside!*

Contrast: **clean, pure, immaculate, spotless; TIDY**

DISHONEST (23)

Dishonest: given to lying, cheating or stealing: *a **dishonest** trader; **dishonest** dealings.* Compare:

deceitful: given to lying and deceiving people
> *the **deceitful** girl said the stolen book was a gift*

devious: not straightforward in your behaviour
> *don't trust him – he's a **devious** character!*

hypocritical: pretending to be good, kind, etc., when you are quite the opposite
> *a **hypocritical** smile concealed her hatred*

sly, cunning, crafty, wily and **artful** all suggest using clever but devious means to get what you want
> *a **sly** old devil; even stupid people can be **cunning**; a **crafty** fellow/trick; a **wily** old aristocrat who escaped the guillotine; what an **artful** child!*

Contrast: **honest, sincere, straightforward, candid, frank**

END (24)

End: to bring or come to an end: *the song **ended**; this battle **ended** the war.* Very similar words are:

finish: stresses the last step or ending of a process
> *I have **finished** my book*

complete: to successfully finish a task
> *have you **completed** the list yet?*

conclude: more formal than 'finish' or 'end'
> *the evening **concluded** with the national anthem*

stop: contrasted with 'start': to put an end to a process
> *she **stopped** reading; the train **stopped***

cease: more formal than 'stop', and often more abrupt
> *he **ceased** laughing when he saw her shocked face*

Contrast: **BEGIN; continue**

DESTROY (20)

Destroy: to cause something to become unusable, unrecognisable or nonexistent: *destroyed in the war; destroy someone's self-respect.* Similar words are:

wreck: to batter to pieces
*the ship was **wrecked**; gossip **wrecked** her reputation*
smash: to break into pieces with a violent blow
*felt like **smashing** the television set*
shatter: to break something brittle into tiny jagged pieces
***shattered** the window; **shattered** his hopes*
ruin: to destroy completely, often over some time
*damp **ruined** the wallpaper; age **ruined** her looks*
demolish: to knock down or take to pieces
*they **demolished** the factory; **demolish** an argument*
raze: to destroy something (especially buildings) totally
*the revolutionaries **razed** the palace to the ground*
abolish: to completely do away with something abstract
***abolish** slavery; **abolish** poor working conditions*
eradicate: to destroy thoroughly, as if pulling up by the roots
*we must **eradicate** drug-taking from our society*
exterminate: to destroy or kill off completely
*the settlers almost **exterminated** the wild deer*
obliterate: to wipe out every trace of something
***obliterate** the memory of something; **obliterate** a dirty mark*
annihilate: (the strongest term) to destroy so completely that it cannot be rebuilt or revived
*we now have the power to **annihilate** the human race*

See also: **impair, KILL**
Contrast: **MAKE; preserve, protect**

EXCELLENT (25)

Excellent: very good of its kind: *an **excellent** meal; **excellent** manners.* Compare:

fine: of high quality
>*fine shoes; a fine singer*

first-class: (worthy of) belonging in the top category
>*a first-class hotel; first-class service*

superior: better than is usual or common
>*a superior class of people; superior accommodation*

choice: selected to meet the highest standards
>*choice peaches; a choice location*

perfect: so good it cannot be improved on
>*a perfect day; the perfect setting*

splendid, superb, admirable: general words of praise
>*a splendid tea; superb scenery; an admirable woman*

Contrast: **inferior, poor, second-rate, mediocre**

FAT (26)

Fat: having more flesh than average. Informal and too blunt to be polite: *you are too **fat**.* Compare:

plump: pleasingly round; praising or euphemistic
>*a plump, cheerful woman; plump peaches*

chubby: pleasantly plump, especially of parts of the body
>*chubby fingers; a chubby baby; chubby crayons*

stout: describes people who are fat or heavily built, but usually also strong and healthy
>*a stout butcher; stout pensioners taking exercise*

portly: stout and dignified
>*a portly alderman went slowly down the street*

obese: (formal) so overweight that your health suffers
>*obese people risk getting a heart attack*

See also: **LARGE.** Contrast: **THIN**

FEAR (27)

Fear: the emotion felt in the face of danger. (See also **ANXIETY**.) Fear may describe a weak or strong emotion: *fear* of flying; *fear* of dying. Compare:

fright: an immediate, often brief reaction of fear
   *you gave me a **fright**, suddenly shouting like that!*
alarm: realisation of imminent danger
   *saw with **alarm** a huge wave approaching the ship*
horror: fear and repulsion; fear for others' safety
   *a **horror** of snakes; saw to her **horror** he was dead*
terror: extreme fear for one's personal safety
   *watched in **terror** as the tanks rolled towards them*
panic: uncontrollable fear; terrified, unthinking actions
   *they scattered in **panic** as the bull charged*

Contrast: **fearlessness, assurance; BRAVE**

FLAW (28)

Flaw, fault, blemish and **defect** all describe a weakness which prevents something from being efficient or excellent.

flaw: something basically wrong in what is otherwise sound or perfect
   *a **flaw** in your reasoning; a **flaw** in the marble*
fault: a flaw in one's character, a machine, etc.
   *a **fault** in the computer; her only **fault***
blemish: a small, usually visible imperfection
   *a **blemish** in the material; pimples are a **blemish***
defect: similar to 'fault'
   *the **defects** of a plan; a serious character **defect***
shortcoming: a minor weakness of character; a fault
   *his main **shortcoming** was his unpunctuality*

Contrast: **merit, virtue, quality**

FOOLISH (29)

Foolish: can describe an action or decision contrary to common sense or good judgement: *a **foolish** idea.* Compare:

silly: less formal than 'foolish'
   *it was **silly** to go out without an umbrella*
senseless: stronger and more critical than the above
   *her **senseless** obstinacy; it is **senseless** to try now*
absurd: laughably inappropriate or unreasonable
   *what an **absurd** notion!*
ridiculous, ludicrous: so absurd as to invite scorn or mocking laughter
   *that **ridiculous** hat! a **ludicrous** way to behave*
preposterous: outrageously absurd
   *a **preposterous** suggestion*

Contrast: **sensible, wise, prudent, reasonable**

GIVE (30)

G

Give: a general term for handing something over to someone else: ***give** me my book.* More precise are:

award: to give as a reward for achievement or excellence
   *she was **awarded** the bronze medal*
donate: to make an official or public gift
   *he **donated** a statue to commemorate his father*
present: to hand over in a ceremonious way
   *the mayor **presented** the prizes*
bestow: used when the giver is more important than the recipient
   *the princess **bestowed** a kiss on the little girl*
grant: to give as a favour in answer to a request
   *the king **granted** the rebels a free pardon*

Contrast: **take, accept, receive; keep, retain, hold on to**

GRAND (31)

Grand: suggests dignity and elegance on a large scale: *grand old palaces*. Often interchangeable with **grand** are:

imposing: impressively large, powerful or extensive
*an **imposing** façade; an **imposing** character*
magnificent: giving an impression of splendour or size
***magnificent** elm trees; a **magnificent** silver jug*
stately: stressing dignity and implying handsomeness
*a **stately** progress; **stately** country houses*
majestic: adds a sense of graceful solemnity to 'stately'
*the **majestic** coronation procession; **majestic** swans*
noble: impressively gracious, dignified, and well-proportioned
*his **noble** face; **noble** Greek temples*

Contrast: **unimposing, insignificant**

H HATE (32)

Hate: a feeling of strong dislike and ill will: *hate is a destructive emotion*. **Hate** is an abstract term. Compare:

hatred: particular hate, directed against things or people
*a **hatred** of war; her **hatred** for her father*
loathing: strong hatred, combined with revulsion
*a **loathing** for slimy things; an irrational **loathing***
enmity: the state of being enemies
*the lasting **enmity** between conquerors and conquered*
hostility: openly expressed dislike or hatred
*they stared at the stranger with **hostility***
antagonism: mutual hostility, especially between two different temperaments
***antagonism** between children and strict parents*

Contrast: **LOVE, friendship, friendliness**

HANDLE (33)

Handle is a general word for touching, holding or moving with your hands: *handle with care*. Similar words with more precise meanings include:

clasp, grasp, grip and **clutch:** ways of seizing or holding tightly:

clasp: to hold closely, lovingly or possessively
> *she **clasped** the child to her bosom*

grasp: to seize eagerly, hold firmly
> *the drowning man **grasped** the lifebelt they threw him*

grip: to hold fast and not let go
> *she **gripped** the rail as the wave broke over the ship*

clutch: to hold or seize something tightly as if afraid of losing it
> *he **clutched** his hat as the wind blew harder*

squeeze: to press on two sides, as if to compress something
> *he **squeezed** her hand and said "I'm sorry"*

pinch: to squeeze between finger and thumb, often causing pain
> *stop **pinching** your little brother this minute!*

finger: to touch or feel, often curiously, with the fingers or fingertips
> *she **fingered** the delicate lace with pleasure*

caress: to finger or stroke lovingly and gently
> *he **caressed** her long black hair*

pat: to tap or stroke lightly and gently
> *the visitor **patted** the little boy on the head*

rub: to press on while moving your hand across
> ***rubbed** the silver teapot until it shone*

HAPPY (34)

Happy: a happy person is habitually or temporarily contented and at ease with the world: *a **happy** child; **happy** to see her home again.* The following words express more active satisfaction: the first group describes a mood, the second may describe mood or character and behaviour.

glad: feeling pleasure mixed with gratitude
   *the rescued mountaineer was **glad** to be alive*
delighted: feeling and showing keen pleasure in something
   ***delighted** with her present; **delighted** by the news*
joyful: excited and rejoicing; expressing joy
   *surrounded by a **joyful** crowd welcoming him back*
gleeful: delighted and in high spirits
   *the **gleeful** pupils were let out of school early because the heating had broken down*
elated: stronger than 'joyful' – carried away by one's joy
   ***elated** by her victory, the sprinter forgot to be tired*
ecstatic: stronger than 'elated' – in a state of bliss
   *my parents were **ecstatic** when they heard of our wedding*
jubilant: triumphantly joyful
   ***jubilant** football supporters*

cheerful: habitually happy and optimistic
   *our **cheerful** milkman is always smiling*
lighthearted: happy and carefree
   *a coachload of **lighthearted** holidaymakers*
merry: in very high spirits, enjoying oneself
   *everyone was very **merry** at the party last night*
jolly, jovial: merry, goodhumoured and sociable
   *your **jovial** uncle enjoys meeting people; we are always a **jolly** crowd at Christmas*

Contrast: **SAD**

HIT (35)

Hit and **strike** can mean to give a blow to. **Strike** has a greater range than **hit**, which stresses aim and the forceful arrival of the blow: *he would never **strike** a child; the driver did not mean to **hit** the gatepost*. Words related to **hit** and **strike** include:

slap: to give a quick, sharp blow with the flat of your hand, making a noise
*the angry woman **slapped** his face*

tap: to strike, often more than once, lightly and gently
*she **tapped** timidly on the door; **tapping** on the window*

knock: to tap more loudly, especially at a door
*who is that **knocking** on our door?*

rap: to knock sharply, quickly, loudly and often repeatedly, usually to gain attention
*the chairman **rapped** on the table*

beat: to strike repeatedly and forcefully
***beat** the dust out of a rug; **beat** the drums*

bang: to beat or strike sharply and resoundingly
*don't **bang** your spoon on the table*

thump: to beat or strike with something heavy, making a dull sound
*his boots **thumped** down the corridor; **thump** one's fist on the table*

punch: to strike suddenly with your fist
*she **punched** her attacker in the stomach*

pound: to beat or strike, perhaps repeatedly, with something blunt or heavy
***pound** the spices to a powder*

batter: to beat or strike repeatedly, causing damage or destruction
*the waves **battered** the ship until it broke up*

IMPORTANT (36)

Important: describing people of authority, influence or power: *a Very **Important** Person (VIP)*. Compare:

great: the most general word of this group. It can refer to rank, power, fame, achievement or ability
*the **great** families of England; **great** women writers*
grand: of high rank or great wealth
*the **grand** duke; I feel very **grand** driving this Rolls*
illustrious: enjoying great glory and well-deserved fame
*portraits of his **illustrious** ancestors*
eminent: respected for high rank or attainment
***eminent** scientists have praised her work*
mighty: very powerful and influential
***mighty** rulers of the ancient Eastern empires*

Contrast: **lowly, obscure, unimportant, unknown**

INJURE (37)

Injure: to cause something to be less effective or perfect:
***injured** her leg; **injured** our chances*. Compare:

damage: stresses loss of value, soundness or usefulness
*the scandal **damaged** her reputation; **damaged** crops*
impair: to weaken or lessen in value, efficiency, etc.
***impaired** hearing; tiredness **impaired** his judgement*
harm: stressing the causing of pain or loss
*he wouldn't **harm** a fly; nothing can **harm** her now*
hurt: stresses what is hurt, or the pain or loss itself
***hurt** his leg in the fall; **hurt** her feelings*
mar: stresses the loss of perfection or beauty
*untidiness **marred** your essay; freckles **mar** his face*
spoil: stronger than 'mar', suggesting irreparable damage
*finding a fly in her soup **spoilt** her appetite*

Contrast: **improve, restore; preserve, conserve**

KILL (38)

Kill: a general term meaning to take life: *kill a fly; killed in a car crash.* More specific terms are:

murder: to kill someone deliberately
> *he **murdered** his aunt for her fortune*

execute: to carry out an official sentence of death
> *three men were **executed** for desertion*

slay: (written) to kill violently and deliberately
> *St George **slew** the dragon*

assassinate: to murder for political reasons
> *the Prime Minister has been **assassinated***

butcher: to kill brutally and messily
> *the murderer **butchered** his victims with an axe*

slaughter: to kill violently, bloodily or in huge numbers
> *thousands were **slaughtered** in the battle*

massacre: to slaughter numbers of defenceless people
> *the enemy soldiers **massacred** the villagers*

See also: **DESTROY**. Contrast: **spare; save life**

KIND (39)

Kind, kindly: treating others with kindness, mercy and compassion: *a **kind** heart; **kind** neighbours; a **kindly** smile.* Similar words are:

kindhearted: kind by nature
> *my **kindhearted** old teacher listened sympathetically*

gracious: courteous and kind, especially to inferiors
> *the queen bent towards the child with a **gracious** smile*

benevolent: full of goodwill towards others
> *a **benevolent** town council gave the youth club a grant*

compassionate: (habitually) full of sympathy or pity
> *two **compassionate** sisters who tend injured animals*

Contrast: **CRUEL; unkind, spiteful, malicious**

L **LARGE (40)**

Large: of greater than average size, amount or capacity:
  *a **large** garden; **large** quantities of ice cream*
big: often interchangeable with 'large', but less formal
  *a **big** house; a **big** bag; a **big** pile of papers*
great: large in degree; large and imposing
  *a **great** deal of work; a **great** cathedral; a **great** oak door*

Stronger than **large, big** and **great** are:

huge: of very great size, bulk, or capacity
  *a **huge** Easter egg; **huge** cooling towers*
massive: huge in bulk or weight
  *a **massive** wrestler; **massive** iron bolts*
enormous: stronger than 'huge'
  *an **enormous** elephant loomed over us*
vast: very great in range or extent
  ***vast** sheets of ice cover the Arctic landscape*
immense: much greater than average in size or degree
  *the **immense** jungles of Brazil; **immense** vitality*
colossal: awesomely large
  ***colossal** statues, three times larger than life*
gigantic: giant-sized; very great
  ***gigantic** afternoon shadows; **gigantic** problems*
towering: very tall
  ***towering** office blocks; a house dwarfed by **towering** trees*
monumental: very large in degree (informal) or importance
  ***monumental** ignorance; a **monumental** study of rabies*

Contrast: **SMALL**

LAUGH (41)

Laugh: to express amusement or happiness with facial gestures and explosive sounds: *they **laughed** at the clown until they cried.* Related words include:

chuckle: to laugh quietly to yourself in amused appreciation
>*we **chuckled** at the cartoon in this morning's paper*

giggle: to laugh in short bursts in a high-pitched, rather silly and childish way
>*girls **giggling** together in a corner*

titter: to giggle nervously or affectedly
>*the class **tittered** as the teacher read them a love poem*

snigger: (especially of children) to let out half-suppressed giggles of derisive amusement
>*the boys **sniggered** as she slipped on the ice*

guffaw: to let out great bursts of hearty, unrestrained laughter
>*we could hear the men **guffawing** in the next room*

smile: to turn up the corners of your mouth in an expression of pleasure, friendliness or amusement
>*she **smiled** at us and said "Do come in"*

smirk: to smile in a self-satisfied kind of way
>*the politician **smirked** at the photographers*

grin: to give a broad, spontaneous smile of pleasure or friendliness
>*she **grinned** as she saw us approaching*

beam: to grin widely to express joy or goodwill
>*the minister **beamed** at his congregation*

See also: **HAPPY**. Contrast: **CRY**

LOUD (42)

Loud: describing sound of high volume or intensity: *turn down the radio – it's too **loud***. More precise words are:

piercing: high-pitched and penetrating
> *her **piercing** voice sent shivers down his spine*

ringing: clear and resounding
> *"I will never agree to treachery," she said in **ringing** tones*

booming: loud and resonant
> *his voice **boomed** down the corridor like a foghorn*

strident: insistently loud and harsh
> *the bar was full of men with **strident** voices*

shrill: sharp and high-pitched, like children's voices
> *a **shrill** scream echoed through the castle*

Contrast: **faint, low, hushed, muted, quiet, inaudible**

LOVE (43)

Love, fondness, affection and **devotion** all suggest warm feelings of regard and tenderness.

devotion: loving loyalty and service
> ***devotion** to duty; a father's **devotion** to his child*

affection: kind and tender feelings for someone
> *her **affection** for the old lady grew daily*

fondness: a strong liking for something or someone
> *a **fondness** for children/chocolates*

love: the strongest term, describing feelings from deep affection to passionate or spiritual devotion
> ***love** of one's country; **love** for a wife/husband/friend*

Contrast: **HATE, dislike; indifference**

MAKE (44)

Make: a general word for causing something to exist: ***make*** *a cake/a mistake/friends/a plan*. Compare:

create: suggests artistic or intelligent purpose
   create *a work of art/a home/a new understanding*
construct: to build or create in a well thought-out way
   construct *a house/a theory/a model railway*
form: implies that what is made has a structure or shape
   *we **formed** a ring round them; **form** it into a ball*
fashion: suggests creativity or ingenuity
   *she **fashioned** a sling from her scarf*
produce: stresses the result rather than the process
   *the factory **produced** more goods than ever this year*

Contrast: **DESTROY**

MANY (45)

Many: large in numbers of like things: ***many*** *poets;* ***many*** *hats;* ***many*** *ideas.* Less general than **many** are:

numerous: like 'many', but stressing the individual units
   *visited on **numerous** occasions; **numerous** hotels*
multifarious: many and different
   *her **multifarious** interests include reading and golf*
frequent: occurring many times
   frequent *stops for coffee;* ***frequent*** *visitors*
countless: too many to count
   countless *as the stars*
plentiful: (of things) more than enough
   plentiful *supplies; vegetables are **plentiful** this year*
abundant: plentiful (of abstract or growing things)
   *blackberries are **abundant** now; **abundant** ideas*

Contrast: **few, infrequent, scarce, rare, sparse**

N NEW (46)

New: made, found, etc. recently, not existing before: *a new theory; a new coat; new neighbours.* Compare:

original: the first of its kind, or a new way of doing something
an original idea; the original model
fresh: suggests the qualities associated with newness: youthfulness, vigour, brightness
fresh paint; a fresh look at the classics
novel: new and unfamiliar, strange or striking
a novel method of saving energy

Contrast: **OLD**

O OBVIOUS (47)

Obvious: not difficult to see or understand: *the answer is obvious; her obvious dismay.* Similar words are:

evident: obvious from the circumstances or the facts
it was evident that she would soon be well again
apparent: becoming obvious after interpreting the signs
it soon became apparent that their visitor had fallen asleep
clear, plain: easy to see or understand; unmistakable
*a clear case of mistaken identity; the path was clear;
it was plain that she would answer no more questions*
distinct: so sharply defined that it can easily be seen, heard, felt, etc.
felt a distinct bump on my forehead; a distinct voice
lucid: (of writing, explanations, etc.) clear and logical
a lucid explanation; a lucid writer

Contrast: **obscure, puzzling; concealed, SECRET**

OLD (48)

Old: describing people, things, ideas which have been known or in existence for a long time: *my old friends; an old horse; old clothes.* More precise than **old** are:

ancient: belonging to the distant past; very old
>   *the ancient Greeks; an ancient car rattled past*
antique: of the more recent past and valued for its age
>   *she collects antique furniture*
antiquated: old but not valued; out-of-date
>   *an antiquated washing machine; antiquated ideas*
elderly: (of people) past middle age but not yet old
>   *her elderly parents are still very active*

Contrast: **NEW**

PASSIONATE (49)

P

Passionate: showing or driven by strong emotion:
passionate pleas; a passionate lover. Similar are:

ardent, fervent: burning with intense emotion
>   *an ardent admirer; a fervent believer*
vehement: energetic and forceful (not used of people)
>   *a vehement denial; vehement debates*
zealous: untiringly enthusiastic, especially in the service of
>   a cause
>   *made zealous efforts to convert the local people*
enthusiastic: feeling and expressing intense admiration or
>   eagerness for or about something
>   *an enthusiastic member of the sailing club*
eager: feeling a strong desire or impatience for
>   *eager to see his old friend/the ancient city*

See also: **ACTIVE.** Contrast: **apathetic, impassive**

POOR (50)

Poor: not having enough money or possessions to live in reasonable comfort: *poor families; poor areas of London.* The following words tell us more:

needy: lacking even necessities; very poor
    needy refugee families living in camps
deprived: a modern euphemism for 'poor'
    the deprived children of our slums
penniless: having no money (often temporarily)
    I spent my last pound on the train ticket and arrived in London penniless
destitute: totally without resources
    the earthquake left hundreds of people destitute

Contrast: **rich, affluent, wealthy, prosperous, well-off**

PROUD (51)

Proud can mean having or showing too great a belief in your own superiority: *too proud to speak to us.* Compare:

arrogant: insolent, overbearing and self-important
    an arrogant youth started ordering us around
haughty: conscious of your own superior birth or status
    the haughty duchess ignored our friendly greeting
supercilious: disdainful, proud and aloof
    a supercilious smile; supercilious shop assistants
vain: filled with admiration for yourself, and wishing to impress others, especially with your looks
    the vain young girl was flattered by his praises
conceited: having too high an opinion of yourself
    the conceited child was boasting of his high marks

Contrast: **humble, modest, self-deprecating**

PULL (52)

Pull: to move, or try to move, something along behind you: *a child **pulling** a toy horse on wheels*. Similar are:

draw: to pull smoothly and easily
> *she **drew** her stool closer to the fire*

drag: to pull something heavy or which resists being moved
> *they **dragged** logs home from the forest*

haul: to pull something heavy, slowly and steadily
> *it took two engines to **haul** the train*

tow: to pull using a rope or chain
> *a patient horse **towed** the barge*

tug: to give short, energetic pulls, which do not necessarily result in any movement
> *she **tugged** her father's sleeve until he looked round*

PUSH (53)

Push: to move, or try to move, something forwards in front of you: ***push** the door and it will open*. Compare:

shove: (informal) to push roughly or hastily
> *let's **shove** the box out of sight under the bed*

thrust: to push energetically or suddenly, often into or out of something
> *the little boy **thrust** his hands into his pockets*

drive: to send forwards (or downwards) purposefully and forcefully
> *the footballer **drove** the ball into the net*

propel: to send forwards rapidly (as if) by a machine
> *the wind **propelled** us along the beach*

manhandle: to move something big and awkward, by human strength
> ***manhandling** the heavy barrels down the cellar steps*

QUICK (54)

Quick, fast, rapid and swift all describe things done
at speed, or moving at speed. They are often interchangeable.

quick: taking a very short time
    a **quick** look at the paper; a **quick** worker
fast: used especially of things or people carrying out
    continuous actions
    a **fast** train; a **fast** runner
rapid: used especially for a series of quick actions, or
    uninterrupted progress
    a **rapid** calculation; a **rapid** recovery
swift: the most formal and literary word, it suggests speed
    and smoothness, especially in people or animals
    the **swift** flight of swallows; a **swift** look round to see
    they had left nothing behind

Brisk, spry, agile and nimble can describe someone who
moves quickly and easily:

brisk: suggests quickness, energy and often efficiency
    a **brisk** walk; a **brisk** manner; a **brisk** salesman
spry: active and in good health, in spite of one's age
    a **spry** old lady who still cycles to the shops
agile: athletic, supple and even graceful in body or mind
    agile mountain climbers; an **agile** mind is useful in
    business
nimble: moving lightly, rapidly and skilfully
    nimble fingers; the **nimble** child was soon at the top of
    the tree

See also: **RUN, ACTIVE**
Contrast: **slow, gradual, leisurely; torpid, sluggish**

REBUKE (55)

Rebuke: to criticise sharply or sternly for a fault: *she rebuked her son for telling lies*. Other words for expressing strong disapproval or criticism include:

reproach: implies a personal grievance, and aims to make someone ashamed of thoughtless or selfish behaviour
he reproached her for failing to write to him
reprove: to criticise mildly with the aim of correcting the fault
the teacher reproved the boy for talking in class
reprimand: to give a severe, formal or public rebuke
the officer was reprimanded by his commander
scold: (usually of elders or superiors) to rebuke at length and abusively in an irritated way
she scolded her children for staying out late

Contrast: **praise, commend, approve**

REQUEST (56)

Request: a courteous or formal alternative for 'ask': *we request the pleasure of your company*. The following stronger words suggest more urgency:

appeal: to make a humble and earnest request
the prisoner appealed for mercy
plead: stronger and more emotional than appeal
the distraught woman pleaded to see her children
beg: to ask for as a supplicant, earnestly and repeatedly
she begged me to come; he begs for your forgiveness
entreat, beseech (formal), **implore:** (in increasing order of urgency) to make urgent and emotional appeals
*entreated him, for the sake of his health, not to go;
I beseech you to remember your sacred vow;
weeping bitterly, she implored him to return soon*

Contrast: **demand, require, claim; order, command**

RUN (57)

Run: to move rapidly forward on foot: *he **ran** down the road*.
Words which suggest speedy movement include:

rush: suggests haste and lack of care
   * **rushed** out of the room in tears*
dash: suggests haste and lack of restraint
   * **dashed** across the road after her*
race: to move rapidly and continuously
   * **raced** down the street; a **racing** river*
sprint: to race at full speed for a short distance
   * **sprinting** for a bus*
dart: to move suddenly and with speed
   * the lad **darted** down an alleyway and disappeared*
scamper: to run (about) with the quick, agile movements of a
small animal
   * the children **scampered** back to bed*
scurry: very similar, but suggesting more haste
   * the squirrel **scurried** up a tree when it saw us*
scuttle: similar but suggesting awkward movements
   * the bent little woman **scuttled** off with our tickets*
fly: to move as swiftly as if through the air
   * time **flies**; "I must **fly**," she cried, "or I'll be late"*
scud: to move lightly and rapidly like racing clouds
   * a yacht **scudding** before the wind*
streak: to move almost too fast to be seen
   * the racehorse **streaked** past the finishing post*
hurtle: to rush violently, noisily or dangerously
   * we clung on tightly as the sledge **hurtled** down the hill*

See also: **QUICK**. Contrast: **WALK**

SAD (58)

Sad: a general term for being unhappy or in low spirits. It can vary from temporary unhappiness to great misery: *sad mourners*; *sad to say goodbye*. Compare:

dejected, downcast: temporarily discouraged
  dejected wallflowers at the party
  too cheerful a person to be downcast for long
despondent, depressed: disheartened and hopeless
  lines of despondent people without work;
  depressed when publishers kept returning her novel
glum: silent and depressed
  his glum face told me he had not got the job
gloomy: in low spirits; pessimistic in outlook
  the treasurer's report made the committee gloomy
dismal: cheerless and depressing
  cheer up! Take that dismal expression off your face!
doleful, mournful: expressing sadness
  we couldn't help laughing at her doleful expression
  when she found the cat had eaten her supper; the
  child's mournful face inspired us with pity
melancholy: sad and thoughtful
  melancholy poets, writing about death
miserable, wretched: suffering from grief or depression
  I was miserable for weeks when my grandfather died;
  the wretched mother watched her child growing
  thinner
inconsolable, heartbroken: too sad to be comforted
  the girl who lost her puppy was inconsolable;
  the jilted lover was heartbroken
sorrowful: very sad, in a quiet, dignified way
  the sorrowful parents followed the coffin
griefstricken: overwhelmed by grief or remorse
  offered sympathy to the griefstricken widow

See also: **SUFFERING**. Contrast: **HAPPY**

SAY (59)

Say: to pronounce words: *did he **say** that?* Often interchangeable with **say** or each other are:

utter: stresses the act of saying words or making sounds
  *could not **utter** a word; **utters** a cry of horror*
express: to put into words
  *how can I **express** my thanks?*
speak: to express your thoughts in uttered words
  ***speak** to us about your experiences in the jungle*
state: suggests making a statement, speaking clearly
  *she **stated** her terms for letting the room*
declare: to state positively and openly or publicly
  *he **declared** that nothing would stop him*
assert: to state positively, in the face of possible denial, something one believes to be true
  *she **asserted** that the window had always been broken*
announce: to declare (especially something new)
  ***announced** their engagement; **announced** that she was leaving immediately*
proclaim: to declare loudly, boldly, formally
  ***proclaimed** him king; she **proclaimed** her innocence*
tell: stresses communicating ideas by speaking
  ***tell** us why you did it; **tell** us about your family*
recount: to give a careful, detailed account of something
  *he **recounted** his difficulties in getting a visa*
relate: to tell (like) a story; to give an account of
  *she **related** how she had come to live here*
talk: to speak to or in the presence of other people
  *I want to **talk** to you about that job*
chat: to talk together informally and in a friendly way
  *we **chatted** for hours on the phone yesterday*
gossip: to chat and exchange local or trivial information
  *I must stop **gossiping** and get back to work*
chatter: to talk continuously about nothing very much
  *I like John, but he does **chatter** a lot*

SEE (60)

See: to become conscious of through your eyes: *I can **see** you.* Other words for seeing or using your eyes include:

perceive: more formal or literary than 'see'
> *at length she **perceived** a cab approaching*

notice: to have brought to your attention by seeing it
> *he **noticed** a hat lying on the table*

discern: to make out or distinguish, with difficulty
> *they finally **discerned** the lights of the harbour*

glimpse: see briefly; catch sight of
> *we **glimpsed** the Queen as she got into her car*

Look: to use your eyes
> *can we stop and **look** at the view? **Look**, it's lovely!*

gaze: to look at for a long time, in admiration, wonder, awe, etc.
> *we sat **gazing** at the sunset*

stare: to look at fixedly in astonishment, curiosity, etc.
> *he **stared** at her for so long that she began to blush*

gape: to stare at stupidly or in amazement
> *we all **gaped** at the beautiful diamond ring*

peer: to look at closely and with difficulty
> *my mother **peered** short-sightedly at the letter*

glance at: to look at briefly or hurriedly
> *she **glanced** at her watch and said she had to go*

scan: to move your eyes across in order to examine
> *the admiral **scanned** the horizon with his binoculars*

survey: to take a broad, general look at a scene
> *she **surveyed** the faces round the dinner table*

watch: to look at attentively for some time
> ***watch** the dancing; **watch** the door until he comes out*

observe: to watch intently and like a scientist
> ***observed** the arrival of the winter migrants*

SECRET (61)

Secret may describe behaviour or actions intentionally hidden from others: *secret smoking.* Compare:

covert: stresses the lack of openness
    *a **covert** yawn; **covert** criticism of his friend*
furtive: behaving in a secretive or underhand way because you are ashamed or nervous
    *she stole a **furtive** look at her sister's letters*
stealthy: moving cautiously so as to avoid notice
    *he followed his victims with **stealthy** steps*
surreptitious: seizing opportunities to indulge in behaviour disapproved of or forbidden
    *a **surreptitious** look at a comic during lessons*

Contrast: **open, undisguised, overt, explicit; OBVIOUS**

SERIOUS (62)

Serious may describe responsible people who do not treat matters too lightly: *a **serious** writer.* Similar words are:

grave: very serious; concerned about important matters
    *the doctor looked **grave** as she left her patient*
solemn: serious and dignified through awe or grief
    ***solemn** faces at the funeral*
sober: calm, composed, not easily excited
    *a **sober** man whose chief pleasure was classical music*
staid: correct, respectable, restrained and rather prim
    *a **staid** old lady who disapproves of modern manners*
earnest: intensely and purposefully serious and keen
    ***earnest** students were discussing their research*

Contrast: **light, flippant, frivolous, irresponsible**

SHINE (63)

Shine: to give out or reflect a steady light: *the sun is **shining** today.*

Glow, gleam and **glisten** also suggest a steady light:

glow: to give out light from within, often with a suggestion of warmth
*the **glow** of a dying fire*
gleam: to give a steady but subdued light, often against a dark background
*the pewter pots **gleamed** in the firelight*
glisten: describes light reflected from a wet or shiny surface
*freshly caught fish **glistened** in the pail*

Flicker, glint, glitter, sparkle, shimmer and **twinkle** suggest an unsteady light, or one that is not continuous:

flicker: to give a little, fluctuating light
*the candlelight **flickered** over his face*
glint: of bright, reflected light that comes and goes
*the cars in the traffic jam **glinted** in the sun*
glitter: to continually flash light from many different points
*the diamonds **glittered** temptingly before her eyes*
sparkle: like 'glitter', but inviting and pleasing where 'glitter' may suggest evil intentions
*her eyes **sparkled** with pleasure when she saw them*
twinkle: of small points of light – to shine brightly but unsteadily
*the moon shone and the stars **twinkled** above*
shimmer: to give a gentle, moving light, like that reflected from water or smooth materials
*moonlight **shimmered** on the waves; the silk scarf **shimmered** in the candlelight*

See also: **BRIGHT**

SHOW (64)

Show: to allow or cause something to be visible: *show me your hands*. The following are ways of showing:

reveal: to show as if by drawing back a veil
*the curtain rose to **reveal** a woodland scene*
disclose: to show something formerly hidden or secret
*she opened her hands and **disclosed** a tiny bird*
expose: to show something normally hidden
*the tide had gone out, **exposing** the rock pools*
display: to put on show, to show to advantage
*he **displayed** his pebble collection in a glass case*
flaunt: to show something off in order to mock or insult
***flaunted** her furs in the face of her poor relations*

Contrast: **conceal, hide; SECRET**

SKILFUL (65)

Skilful: possessing natural ability, improved by training and experience: *a **skilful** debater/craftswoman*. Often interchangeable with **skilful** and with each other are:

adroit: quick and effective; clever at handling situations
*an **adroit** change of subject; an **adroit** fielder*
deft: suggests (especially manual) skill without effort
*a **deft** knitter; a **deft** kick sent the ball into the net*
adept: having a natural talent improved by practice
*she is **adept** at telling stories/balancing accounts*
proficient: very competent due to training and practice
*a **proficient** typist/pianist/linguist*

See also: **CLEVER**. Contrast: **awkward, clumsy, maladroit, inept**

SMALL (66)

Small: of less than average size or amount. Unlike **little** it often implies a comparison: *we only want a **small** house; a **small** helping of custard; a **small** child should not be left on her own.*

Little: often interchangeable with **small**. It can also suggest affection or pettiness: *We love **little** children; **little** things please **little** minds.*

More precise words which may replace **small** or **little** include:

tiny: very small. It often suggests affection
>*look at Baby's **tiny** fingers*

miniature: on a small scale
>*a **miniature** tea set for the dolls' house*

petite: of women or girls: having a small, trim figure
>*an attractive style for the **petite** woman*

dainty: small and delicate
>***dainty** fingers; **dainty** china cups; a **dainty** figure*

diminutive: exceptionally or abnormally small
>*from the fifteenth floor we could see **diminutive** figures walking in the street far below*

minute: even smaller; difficult to see
>*a **minute** crack in the engine caused the explosion*

microscopic: smaller still; literally, invisible to the naked eye
>***microscopic** creatures live in pond water*

Contrast: **LARGE**

SMELL (67)

Smell: the general term for something that you can smell, whether it is pleasant or unpleasant: *a **smell** of onions/cooking/wet fur.* Alternative words include:

odour: a close equivalent of 'smell', but more formal
> *the unmistakable **odour** of ripe apples*
scent: a delicate, pleasant smell
> *the **scent** of new-mown hay*
perfume: the pleasant smell we associate with flowers
> *the heady **perfume** of lilies*
fragrance: similar to 'perfume', but especially suggesting lightness and delicacy
> *the sweet **fragrance** of violets; had her own **fragrance***
aroma: an agreeable, spicy or pungent smell
> *delicious **aromas** wafted out of the kitchen*
stench: a very strong, offensive smell of filth or decay
> *the **stench** of blocked drains*

STRANGE (68)

Strange: something or someone unusual or unexpected. Similar words include:

curious, peculiar: different from normal in a way that arouses interest or surprise
> ***curious** old carvings; a **peculiar** twisted smile*
queer, odd: (often critical) unconventional or abnormal
> ***queer** neighbours; **odd** behaviour*
weird: contrasted with ordinary, everyday reality
> *a **weird** experience; the **weird** beauty of the moon*
eccentric: very odd
> *the **eccentric** old lady keeps forty cats*
bizarre: sensationally strange
> ***bizarre** feather head-dresses*

Contrast: **ordinary, familiar, normal, usual, conventional**

STIR (69)

Stir: to make slight movements: *the leaves **stirred** in the breeze.* More agitated movement is suggested by:

shake: suggests rapid, irregular movement that may be quite violent
    *the houses **shook** as a bomb burst nearby*
vibrate: suggests rapid, continuous, rhythmical movements
    *the rails **vibrated** as the train approached*
quiver: to vibrate rapidly and almost invisibly; in people it suggests involuntary, apprehensive shaking
    *her heart **quivered** as she knocked at the door; the arrow **quivered** in the tree trunk*
quake: to shake convulsively; used of people, it suggests fear, nervousness, weakness, etc.
    *I was **quaking** in my shoes when I knew they had found out; the ground **quaked** as the tanks rolled forward*
tremble: usually used of people, it suggests involuntary shaking because of fear, nervousness, cold, weakness or strong emotion
    *he **trembled** with fear and cold as he waited for dawn*
shiver: like 'tremble', but especially suggesting cold
    *poor tramps **shivering** round a tiny fire*
shudder: usually used of people, it suggests a convulsive movement of dislike or repulsion
    *the girl **shuddered** as the snake slid forward*

Rock: describes the unsteady rocking motion of something big or topheavy: *the old house **rocked** in the winter gales.* Compare:

totter: to rock or move forward as if about to fall or collapse. In people, it suggests age or weakness
    *the bulldozed building **tottered** then collapsed*
wobble: like 'rock', but used of things that are not solid, or which are badly balanced
    *jelly **wobbles**; this table **wobbles***

STRONG (70)

Strong: describes what is powerful, able to exert force, or to withstand ill-treatment: ***strong*** *wrestlers; a* ***strong*** *box.* Words which describe kinds of strength include:

solid: substantial, made of a heavy or durable material
    the seat looked ***solid****, but it collapsed when she sat on it*
tough: able to withstand rough treatment or hardship; possessing stamina and powers of endurance
    a ***tough*** *skin; soldiers training to be* ***tough***
indestructible: too strong to be destroyed
    they thought the ship ***indestructible***
stout, sturdy: suggests solidity and durability, and in people, stockiness, resoluteness or rugged good health
    a ***stout*** *lad;* ***stout****-hearted;* ***sturdy*** *legs/furniture*
stalwart: (people) well-built, big, strong and resolute
    stalwart *Highlanders of the Queen's Guard*
strapping: (people) well-developed, sturdy and strong
    strapping *young men sprawling in the sun*
muscular: (mainly people) strong and well-built, with powerful muscles
    muscular *athletes throwing the hammer*
burly: (people) having an unusually large, powerful body with well-developed muscles
    burly *bodyguards are always by his side*
robust: (of living things) vigorously healthy or tough
    a ***robust*** *oak tree;* ***robust*** *young footballers*
hardy: (of living things) able to endure bad weather, hardship, etc.
    hardy *old seadogs;* ***hardy*** *plants for cold climates*

Contrast: **WEAK**

SUCCEED (71)

Succeed: to successfully reach an objective: *succeeded in learning some French/getting the job.* Compare:

achieve: to carry out or obtain in the face of difficulties
*   **achieve** one's heart's desire; **achieve** the impossible*
accomplish: stresses the successful completion of a task
*   he **accomplished** what he set out to do*
attain: to reach a desirable end through one's efforts
*   in time she **attained** the premiership/peace of mind*
win: to obtain after a struggle
*   **win** recognition/a place in the team/all our hearts*

See also: **END.** Contrast: **fail; lose; give up**

SUFFERING (72)

Suffering: mental or physical pain or discomfort: *after much suffering, she recovered.* Stronger words include:

distress: showing signs of being upset or anxious
*   his **distress** on learning the news was obvious*
misery: longstanding unhappiness and wretchedness
*   the **misery** of drug addiction*
sorrow: deep sadness; a sense of loss
*   we learned of his death with **sorrow***
grief: keen sorrow for something in particular
*   she thought she would die of **grief** when he left her*
anguish: almost unbearable mental suffering
*   the **anguish** of having to leave her lifelong home*

See also: **SAD, ANXIETY.** Contrast: **joy, pleasure, delight**

THIN (73)

Thin: may describe people who have little flesh on them, often to an unnatural degree: *a thin child who refuses to eat.* Words which may replace **thin** include:

slim: acceptably thin, having a trim figure, perhaps through having gone on a diet
*she would like to be **slim**, but can't resist cakes*

slender: of slight build, but also lithe or graceful
*her **slender** frame moved gracefully to the music*

spare: with no excess fat, but strong and vigorous
*the **spare** figure of a cowboy*

lean: acceptably thin (especially used of men); like 'spare', it also suggests vigour and strength
*the **lean**, sunburnt faces of men who work out of doors*

wiry: thin, but tough and sinewy
*a **wiry** little woman who had brought up ten children*

lanky: tall and thin, awkward and graceless
***lanky** youths may grow into tall and handsome men*

skinny: (informal) an uncomplimentary description of someone who is thought to be too thin
*she was once a **skinny** little girl with pigtails*

scrawny: also uncomplimentary, as it is used to describe animals and plants, too
***scrawny** little beggar children, scrounging crusts*

gaunt: thin and bony; haggard-looking as a result of suffering or illness
*the patient's **gaunt** face; **gaunt** desert wanderers*

emaciated: gaunt through lack of food or illness
*haunting photographs of **emaciated** refugees*

Contrast: **FAT**

THINK (74)

Think: to turn something over in your mind: ***think*** *about getting a new job.* These words are more precise:

consider: to think carefully about large or small matters
> ***consider*** *whether to get married/ have some more tea*
weigh (up): to consider all aspects of something
> *after **weighing** the evidence, the jury found him guilty*
deliberate: to think deeply and for a long time before making a decision
> *we **deliberated** whether to increase our fees*
ponder: to think deeply and seriously about something
> *she **pondered** her mother's words*
meditate: to spend some time in concentrated thought
> *the repentant murderer **meditated** on his crime*

TIDY (75)

Tidy: orderly, clean, pleasing to the eye: *a **tidy** room; a **tidy** desk; **tidy** hair.* Compare:

spotless, immaculate: tidy and very clean
> *a **spotless** kitchen; **immaculate** white shirts*
neat: (of people and things) simple and orderly
> ***neat** white socks; **neat** handwriting*
trim: neat and compact or precise
> ***trim** waiters; a **trim** figure*
shipshape: efficiently tidy
> *I like to keep my desk **shipshape***
spick and span: immaculate and in good order
> *a **spick and span** bachelor flat*
spruce, dapper: (people) smartly and neatly dressed
> ***spruce** young men out with their girlfriends;*
> *a **dapper** little fellow in a yellow jacket*

Contrast: **untidy, unkempt, dishevelled, bedraggled, DIRTY**

THROW (76)

Throw: to send flying through the air with your arm: *throw me the ball.* **Throw** may be replaced by:

cast: now literary, except in certain phrases
  *fishermen **cast** their nets; **cast** doubts on his honesty*
toss: to throw lightly up into the air
  *the audience **tossed** flowers onto the stage*
sling: to throw with a quick, sweeping movement
  *she **slung** her schoolbag into the corner*
fling: to throw violently, often because of emotion
  *he **flung** himself onto the bed and wept bitterly*
hurl: to throw with great force at something
  ***hurled** a stone at the window*

UNPLEASANT (77)

Unpleasant: disagreeable, displeasing or disliked: *an **unpleasant** smell/task/habit.* Stronger words include:

nasty: very unpleasant, e.g. to smell or to taste
  *a **nasty** mess; **nasty** medicine*
horrid: (informal) causing strong dislike; repugnant
  *what a **horrid** tie/colour/taste/picture/experience*
repulsive: (especially of ugliness or crude behaviour)
  causing disgust; repellent
  *the Beast's **repulsive** features did not frighten Beauty*
revolting: causing shock, disgust and even nausea
  *what a **revolting** film! It made me feel quite sick*
loathsome: hateful and repulsive
  *she thinks toads are **loathsome** creatures*
abominable: deservedly hated; morally offensive
  ***abominable** behaviour; an **abominable** criminal*

Contrast: **pleasant, agreeable, delightful, charming, attractive.**

WALK (78)

Walk: to go on foot, without running: ***walk*** *to the station.* Ways of walking include:

stroll: to walk in a leisurely way, perhaps stopping from time to time
*shall we **stroll** down to the park to hear the band?*
saunter: to walk along in a carefree, casual or idle way
***sauntering** along as if there was plenty of time*
amble: to walk in an easy, leisurely way
*when he saw us, he **ambled** over to say hello*
stride: to take long, purposeful and energetic steps
*she **strode** over to the door and flung it open*
strut: to walk in a proud, self-important way
*the little boy was **strutting** up and down in his father's uniform*
plod: to walk slowly, deliberately or heavily
*the backpackers **plodded** on down the road*
trudge: to plod wearily but steadily
*the postwoman **trudged** through the snow*
shuffle: to move along, hardly lifting your feet
*the old tramp **shuffled** along in his ancient boots*
shamble: to move clumsily, usually with your back bent
*a tall, skinny youth **shambled** over to take our order*
hobble: to walk with difficulty (as if) in pain or lame
*she **hobbled** home and kicked off the painful shoes*
stagger: to move forward unsteadily and jerkily
*the wounded guard **staggered** to the alarm bell*
lurch: like 'stagger', but more violent or sudden
*a drunk **lurched** towards them out of the shadows*
reel: to lurch or stagger, as if dizzy
*unbalanced by the blow, she **reeled** across the room*

Contrast: **RUN**

WEAK (79)

Weak: may describe things or people lacking normal strength: *a **weak** heart/argument/kitten.* Compare:

feeble: pathetically weak or inferior
   *a **feeble** cry; a **feeble** attempt; a **feeble** teacher*
decrepit: in poor condition; weakened by age or worn out
   ***decrepit** old tramps; **decrepit** warehouses*
frail: suggests vulnerability due to weakness
   *her **frail** figure, bent under a huge load; a **frail** boat*
fragile: lovely but delicate and easily broken
   ***fragile** china; a **fragile** friendship*
flimsy: of weak construction, liable to collapse
   *a **flimsy** shelter made of cardboard boxes*

Contrast: **STRONG**

WIT (80)

Wit: clever and amusing remarks which associate ideas in a brilliant, perceptive, ingenious or pointed way: *he expresses himself with **wit** and humour.* Compare:

humour: gentler and broader than wit, it consists of an appreciation and/or expression of what is comic or absurd in the human situation
   *her sense of **humour** helped her to survive*
irony: by stating the opposite of what is really meant, irony stresses the gap between how things should be, and how they really are
   *"thank you for a delicious meal," he said with **irony***
sarcasm: a cruel and harsh form of wit, using taunts and irony to ridicule someone or something
   *a teacher disliked for her use of **sarcasm***
satire: writing, etc. that mocks foolishness or evil using irony, wit and sarcasm
   *he wrote a **satire** on trendy young Londoners*

WORD FINDER

A

B

C

fitting **7**
flaunt **64**
FLAW **28**
flicker **63**
flimsy **79**
fling **76**
fly **57**

gallant **12**
gape **60**
gash **17**
gaunt **73**
gaze **60**
gigantic **40**
giggle **41**
GIVE **30**
glad **34**
glance at **60**
gleam **63**
gleeful **34**
glimpse **60**
glint **63**

hack **17**
HANDLE **33**
handsome **9**
HAPPY **34**
harass **5**
hard **21**
hardy **70**
harm **37**
harsh **18**
HATE **32**

illustrious **36**
immaculate **75**
immense **40**

fondness **43**
foolhardy **12**
FOOLISH **29**
form **44**
foul **22**
fragile **79**
fragrance **67**

glisten **63**
glitter **63**
gloomy **58**
glow **63**
glum **58**
gossip **59**
gracious **39**
grand
  GRAND **31**
grand
  IMPORTANT **36**
grant **30**
grasp **33**
grave **62**

hatred **32**
haughty **51**
haul **52**
hazard **19**
heartbroken **58**
heroic **12**
hew **17**
HIT **35**
hobble **78**
horrid **77**

impair **37**
implore **56**
IMPORTANT **36**

frail **79**
frequent **45**
fresh **46**
fright **27**
furtive **61**
fury **4**

great
  IMPORTANT **36**

G

great
  LARGE **40**
grief **72**
griefstricken **58**
grimy **22**
grin **41**
grip **33**
groan **16**
gruff **8**
grumpy **8**
guffaw **41**

horror **27**
hostility **32**
howl **16**
huge **40**
humour **80**
hurl **76**
hurt **37**
hurtle **57**
hypocritical **23**

H

imposing **31**
inconsolable **58**
indestructible **70**

I

peevish 8
penniless 50
perceive 60
perceptive 15
perfect 25
perfume 67
peril 19
perplexing 21
pester 5
petite 66
petulant 8
picturesque 9
piercing 42
pinch 33

pitfall 19
pitiless 18
plain 47
plead 56
plentiful 45
plod 78
plucky 12
plump 26
ponder 74
POOR 50
portly 26
pound 35
preposterous 29
present 30

pretty 9
proclaim 59
produce 44
proficient 65
profitable 11
propel 53
proper 7
PROUD 51
provoke 5
PULL 52
punch 35
PUSH 53

quake 69
queer 68

QUICK 54
quick-witted 15

quiver 69

Q

R

race 57
radiant 13
rage 4
rap 35
rapid 54
raze 20
REBUKE 55
recount 59
reel 78
relate 59

reprimand 55
reproach 55
reprove 55
repulsive 77
REQUEST 56
resentment 4
respect 3
reveal 64
revolting 77
ridiculous 29

ringing 42
risk 19
robust 70
rock 69
rub 33
ruin 20
RUN 57
rush 57
ruthless 18

SAD 58
sadistic 18
sarcasm 80
satire 80
saunter 78
savage 18
SAY 59
scamper 57

scan 60
scent 67
scold 55
scrawny 73
scream 16
scrupulous 14
scud 57
scurry 57

scuttle 57
SECRET 61
SEE 60
senseless 29
SERIOUS 62
sever 17
shake 69
shamble 78

S

HOW TO USE
A THESAURUS

What is a thesaurus?

A thesaurus is a collection of words grouped together
under headings according to their meanings. Unlike a
dictionary, which gives you the meaning of a word, a
thesaurus offers you several words in which you can
express your meaning.

What is a thesaurus for?

A thesaurus has many uses. It can:
    offer you alternative words, so that you do not keep
      repeating the same one
    remind you of a word you have forgotten
    introduce you to a word you did not know before
    help you find a more suitable word, e.g. a formal
      word rather than a colloquial one, for a formal
      letter
    help you find a more precise term
    increase your knowledge of the English language.

So using a thesaurus can help you to express yourself
more clearly, more interestingly, and more effectively.

How is a thesaurus arranged?

The groups of similar words are linked together in a
logical order:
    Class One: abstract ideas such as time and existence
    Class Two: space, and so shape and movement
    Class Three: the physical universe and living things
    Class Four: the human mind, art, language, etc.
    Class Five: the human will and human actions
    Class Six: the human spirit: morality, emotion, religion

Within each class, groups with similar meanings are

kept together, and cross-references link up words of similar meaning in different groups.

How do I use a thesaurus?

The easiest way is to use the Index. This is a guide to the words and phrases to be found in the book, arranged in alphabetical order. Follow these simple steps:

> look up the word for which you wish to find an alternative in the Index
>
> if you cannot find it, look up a different part of speech, i.e. if you looked up a noun, next try looking up a verb, or an adjective
>
> if you still cannot find it, look up a word of similar meaning. A vague word (e.g. 'ship') is better than a specific word (e.g. 'steamboat').

The word you find will be followed by one or more references, showing you where to look in the text:

> each reference consists of a word in italics (the 'keyword') a number, and a part of speech
>
> the number tells you which numbered group to find in the text
>
> the keyword tells you which paragraph contains your word
>
> if there is more than one reference, the keyword will help you to decide which group is most likely to be the one you want.

Now find the numbered group in the text:

> run your eye down the paragraph headings until you find the one beginning with your keyword. Here you should find plenty of alternatives
>
> each numbered group has paragraphs for different parts of speech. Try using another part of speech for a change
>
> most groups are followed by their opposites. Try

rephrasing what you want to say in the negative cross-references may lead to other useful groups.

Happy word-hunting!